MW00873419

FINDING THE COURAGE TO SAY "I AM"

CHIDELL WATKINS

Publishing
Sherrybrantley.com

FINDING THE COURAGE TO SAY "I AM…"

CHIDELL WATKINS

Michelle,
So nice meeting you and a pleasure! Sitting next to you! Please know that your "I Am's" creative your life. Stay positive. Chidell
609 0057011

Dedication

My life has been full of many twists and turns. This work is dedicated to those of you who have experienced your own twists and turns in life, who at times, wondered 'what am I doing here—and why?' It is my hope that the information in this book will assist you to begin to create the powerful, positive life you've always envisioned for yourself.

I would like to take this time to dedicate this work to my family, friends, mentors, coaches and co-workers, who have spurred me on, encouraged me, uplifted me and believed in my vision long before I could 'see it.'

A special dedication to all of the family and friends that have supported me in assisting me to develop and maintain my personal dream of establishing my inspirational and motivational group, 'Girlfriends Connected.' The Spirit, connection and empowerment this group has afforded me and hundreds of other women has been a very humbling, loving experience for me. I do not take lightly the power of women of good intent, coming together for the betterment of all!

FINDING THE COURAGE TO SAY "I AM…"

CHIDELL WATKINS

TABLE OF CONTENTS

CHIDELL WATKINS

THE POWER OF 'I AM'

The power of I AM… Two powerful words that you can put in front of any sentence, phrase, or group of words to create the life you desire.

Many people talk about the power of saying *I Am,* but it's the *COURAGE* of saying those two words that help in making an impact in our lives. How many times have you heard someone say: *"We know what to do but we don't do it?"* Or how about, *"Oh that stuff doesn't work."* Well, what if you were to try it and it does work? What do you have to lose? I would say if you could take just 10 to 15 minutes out of your day at minimum, to put into practice reciting a positive affirmation, then begin reflecting and acting on that affirmation for the day, it could have a positive and rewarding impact on your life!

What is an affirmation? According to *Miriam-Webster,* an affirmation is the act of affirming. What does it mean to affirm? *Miriam-Webster* defines affirm as to state something is true in a confident way – to show a strong belief in, or dedication to something. Affirmations are positive statements, and to affirm, means to say yes, or to agree. What you repeatedly speak about, or constantly think about—you bring about! Therefore, you ultimately become, or begin to experience those 'creations' in your life.

CHIDELL WATKINS

Words are very powerful and usually what you speak (out loud) or constantly, think about over long periods of time, comes to fruition in your life. It is very important to be mindful / careful of the words you speak, even if you think it is in a joking way. There are a multitude of examples of people saying things or making comments 'just because,' then by surprise, those things actually occur. When you say things like: *"I am broke," "I am not happy," "I am struggling,"* etc. these negative things or *negations* can *manifest* in your life.

I know it may seem like an old cliché, but speaking in a positive manner does have a powerful impact on, and *in* your life. What could positive affirmations accomplish for you in your life? How far would you be able to go once you begin to be consistent in using them? What goals, dreams could you bring to fruition? Why not take a few moments to think about that?

As I drive the highway from one state to another, primarily between California and Arizona, I look at the mountains while I pass by them, and say to myself: *"I Am blessed." I Am* at peace gazing through the windshield with the mountains on each side of me: in the forefront, behind me, and at my side. I think of how beautiful the images are to me of the mountains and the blue skies, coupled with gorgeous white clouds. I reflect: *I Am all that I Am, and who I Am supposed to be.*

It's not always easy to say: "*I Am*," and actually believe what you 'confess' after those powerful two words, but it is very possible, especially if you begin to practice repetition.

What is quite interesting, is we know what to say and we have even witnessed others practicing it, but for some of us, we don't fully believe it will, or could happen for us.

In addition to what you are saying, what are you *thinking?* For in order to say something—you must first THINK it! *Your thoughts have an impact on your life.* Are you thinking positive thoughts or negative ones? Everything and every day is not going to be peaches and cream, butterflies and rainbows; or flowers and stars, however how do you handle those trying moments in life? When 'not so good' things happen in your life, you have the ability and the option to find the positive in even the bad or negative situations. As the saying goes, learn to... 'find the silver lining.'

Change your mindset, thoughts, and your words. Instead of thinking and saying *"I am not worthy,"* say: *"I Am worthy."* Instead of thinking or saying, *'I am not pretty,'* say or think instead: *"I Am beautiful."* Rather than saying *"I am not capable,"*

CHIDELL WATKINS

say, "*I Am capable.*" How about instead of; "*I am not smart enough,*" saying "*I Am smart enough.*"

I Am a survivor! I share this because I know a few men and women who have had some of the following experiences and have succumbed to depression, suicidal tendencies, and/or withdrawing from society or social events.

I have survived molestation, rape, abuse, neglect, rejection, untruths, deceit, betrayal, and hurts, which have certainly encompassed physical, mental, verbal, spiritual and emotional pain. Don't get me wrong, all of these are pretty bad experiences in and of themselves individually—let alone collectively. As a result, I have had moments where I didn't think I could continue living, nor did I want to. I would think: *'What is it all for?'* I went through withdrawals, a feeling of abject darkness engulfing me, not wanting to be around anyone, and even questioned, "*Why me? What did I do to deserve this?*"

No matter what it looked like on the outside or how I felt on the inside, I had to convince myself that there was a reason for this happening to me in my life, and that I must continue to 'live.' I began to say positive things about my life, and to myself. Such as: "*I Am pretty.*" No matter how many times others told me how skinny and ugly I was, I had to convince myself otherwise. What better way to do that than to 'affirm' the opposite of what I was being told? I was even asked by former co-workers, who at the time, didn't think I was *'cute enough'* to get raped. *"Oh you got raped?"* Unfortunately, for a long period of time I believed the girls who were shocked that I was *'worthy'* enough of being raped, were right about me. But once I completed the work to empower myself, I wised up and thought instead: Really?! *'Worthy of being raped?!'* As if that were a badge to wear proudly or an honor that was bestowed upon me!?

To try and hold some sort of sick standard of beauty around such a despicable act, only allowed me to see how twisted the minds of my tormentors were. I realized their lowered level of mentality and spirituality was not where I aspired to be, so I went about changing...ME! Once I picked myself up and left that period of darkness, depression, humility and inner withdrawal behind, I began to recite... " *'I Am'* pretty. " " *'I Am'* cute. " " *'I Am'* beautiful." " *'I Am'* worthy." " *'I Am'* a survivor! "

For the next 30 days, commit to stating a positive affirmation out loud, then write a few sentences to yourself in relation to how you could apply this affirmation in your life. When you have completed the next 30 days, repeat them. Get these positive affirmations ingrained in your spirit, in your system, in your life! Be creative and add affirmations that are not included on the worksheets.

Some people practice saying an affirmation or two in the morning while standing in the mirror as they prepare for their day. It is a good idea to reinforce your affirmation a few times throughout the day as the more you say it, you not only begin to believe it, it also begins to manifest in your life.

Don't be discouraged if you do not see 'immediate results,' just keep reciting and believing. Rome wasn't built in a day, and remember *Thomas the Train* says: "I Think I Can, I Think I Can…"

I AM Beautiful
I AM Special
I AM Kind
I AM Smart
I AM Able
I AM Strong
I AM Powerful
I AM Precious
I AM Intelligent
I AM Loving
I AM Friendly
I AM Happy
I AM Healthy
I AM My Sister's/Brother's Keeper
I AM Wealthy

CHIDELL WATKINS

I AM a King / Queen
I AM Successful
I AM Fearless
I AM Courageous
I AM Worthy
I AM Deserving
I AM Blessed
I AM Amazing
I AM Patient
I AM Forgiving
I AM Peaceful
I AM Better Today Than I Was Yesterday
I AM Valuable
I AM Inspiring To Others
I AM Thankful

BONUS:
I Attract Good Things To Me!

I AM BEAUTIFUL BECAUSE...

_____

_____

_____

_____

_____

_____

_____

_____

_____

_____

_____

I AM SPECIAL BECAUSE...

_____

_____

_____

_____

_____

_____

_____

_____

_____

_____

_____

I AM KIND BECAUSE...

_____

_____

_____

_____

_____

_____

_____

_____

_____

_____

_____

I AM SMART BECAUSE…

_____

_____

_____

_____

_____

_____

_____

_____

_____

_____

_____

I AM ABLE BECAUSE...

_____

_____

_____

_____

_____

_____

_____

_____

_____

_____

I AM STRONG BECAUSE...

_____

_____

_____

_____

_____

_____

_____

_____

_____

_____

_____

I AM POWERFUL BECAUSE...

_____

_____

_____

_____

_____

_____

_____

_____

_____

_____

I AM PRECIOUS BECAUSE...

_____

_____

_____

_____

_____

_____

_____

_____

_____

_____

I AM INTELLIGENT BECAUSE...

_____

_____

_____

_____

_____

_____

_____

_____

_____

_____

_____

I AM LOVING BECAUSE...

_____

_____

_____

_____

_____

_____

_____

_____

_____

_____

I AM FRIENDLY BECAUSE...

_____

_____

_____

_____

_____

_____

_____

_____

_____

_____

I AM HAPPY BECAUSE...

_____

_____

_____

_____

_____

_____

_____

_____

_____

_____

I AM HEALTHY BECAUSE...

_____

_____

_____

_____

_____

_____

_____

_____

_____

_____

I AM MY BROTHER'S/SISTER'S KEEPER BECAUSE...

_____

_____

_____

_____

_____

_____

_____

_____

_____

_____

_____

CHIDELL WATKINS

I AM WEALTHY BECAUSE…

CHIDELL WATKINS

I AM A KING/QUEEN BECAUSE...

_____

_____

_____

_____

_____

_____

_____

_____

_____

_____

CHIDELL WATKINS

I AM SUCCESSFUL BECAUSE...

_____

_____

_____

_____

_____

_____

_____

_____

_____

_____

_____

FINDING THE COURAGE TO SAY "I AM..."

CHIDELL WATKINS

I AM FEARLESS BECAUSE...

_____

_____

_____

_____

_____

_____

_____

_____

_____

_____

_____

I AM COURAGEOUS BECAUSE...

_____

_____

_____

_____

_____

_____

_____

_____

_____

_____

_____

_____

CHIDELL WATKINS

I AM WORTHY ENOUGH BECAUSE…

_____

_____

_____

_____

_____

_____

_____

_____

_____

_____

I AM DESERVING BECAUSE...

_____

_____

_____

_____

_____

_____

_____

_____

_____

_____

_____

FINDING THE COURAGE TO SAY "I AM..."

CHIDELL WATKINS

I AM BLESSED BECAUSE...

_____

_____

_____

_____

_____

_____

_____

_____

_____

_____

_____

FINDING THE COURAGE TO SAY "I AM..."

CHIDELL WATKINS

I AM AMAZING BECAUSE...

_____

_____

_____

_____

_____

_____

_____

_____

_____

_____

_____

I AM PATIENT BECAUSE...

_____

_____

_____

_____

_____

_____

_____

_____

_____

_____

_____

_____

I AM FORGIVING BECAUSE…

_____

_____

_____

_____

_____

_____

_____

_____

_____

_____

_____

_____

I AM AT PEACE BECAUSE…

_____

_____

_____

_____

_____

_____

_____

_____

_____

_____

_____

_____

CHIDELL WATKINS

I AM BETTER TODAY THAN I WAS YESTERDAY BECAUSE...

_____

_____

_____

_____

_____

_____

_____

_____

_____

_____

_____

I AM VALUABLE BECAUSE...

_____

_____

_____

_____

_____

_____

_____

_____

_____

_____

_____

I AM INSPIRING TO OTHERS BECAUSE...

_____

_____

_____

_____

_____

_____

_____

_____

_____

_____

_____

I AM THANKFUL BECAUSE...

_____

_____

_____

_____

_____

_____

_____

_____

_____

_____

CHIDELL WATKINS

I ATTRACT GREAT THINGS TO ME
SUCH AS_____ BECAUSE...

_____

_____

_____

_____

_____

_____

_____

_____

_____

_____

The Universe has a definite design in place. A part that allows us to create and enjoy opportunities that will allow us to experience those things we'd like to experience, so that we are all able to pursue our passionate purpose and our true destinies, on whatever path or journey that may mean for you.

It is not as difficult to release fear, even though many of us have been taught just the opposite. That releasing fear is difficult, challenging, and next to impossible. However, because the Universe is based on positive, affirmative principles, we simply need to *find the courage* to say yes to those things we want to create, and deliver the 'no's,' for the things we no longer want to experience.

After putting these affirmations into practice you will begin to feel very good about yourself as well as see your life change. Like *Dorothy,* in the *Land of Oz,* you've had the courage all along—NOW is simply the time to use it!

ABOUT THE AUTHOR

Chidell Watkins is an author, speaker and keynoter. She is the Founder of the inspiring, *'Girlfriends Connected,'* A nationally recognized group whose mission is to connect women from across the globe, with the intention of facilitating growth in many areas: Personally, physically, financially, mentally and spiritually!

Girlfriends Connected annual, 3-day event supports women in all walks of life to begin to pursue their passionate purpose!

Contact Chidell at:
Girlfriendsconnected4u@gmail.com.
www.girlfriendsconnected4u.com
Twitter @girlfriendsc
Instagram @girlfriendsconnected
FB girlfriendsconnectedaz

48086696R00028

Made in the USA
San Bernardino, CA
16 April 2017